D0359562

Pebble®

I DON'T BULLY

I Am ~~WITHDRAWN~~ Caring

by Melissa Higgins

Consulting Editor: Gail Saunders-Smith, PhD

Content Consultant: Susan M. Swearer, PhD
Professor of School Psychology and Licensed
Psychologist; Co-Director, Bullying Research Network
University of Nebraska–Lincoln

CAPSTONE PRESS
a capstone imprint

Pebble Books are published by Capstone Press,
1710 Roe Crest Drive, North Mankato, Minnesota 56003
www.capstonepub.com

Library of Congress Cataloging-in-Publication Data
Higgins, Melissa, 1953–
I am caring / by Melissa Higgins.
pages cm.—(Pebble books. I don't bully)
Summary: "Simple text and full color photographs describe how to be caring,
not a bully"—Provided by publisher.
Includes bibliographical references and index.
Audience: K to grade 3.
ISBN 978-1-4765-4070-2 (library binding)
ISBN 978-1-4765-5174-6 (paperback)
ISBN 978-1-4765-6039-7 (ebook pdf)
1. Caring in children—Juvenile literature. 2. Aggressiveness in children—Juvenile
literature. 3. Bullying—Prevention—Juvenile literature. I. Title.
BF723.C25H54 2014
177'.7—dc23   2013029370

Note to Parents and Teachers

The I Don't Bully set supports national curriculum standards
for social studies related to people and cultures. This book
describes being caring. The images support early readers
in understanding the text. The repetition of words and
phrases helps early readers learn new words. This book
also introduces early readers to subject-specific vocabulary
words, which are defined in the Glossary section. Early
readers may need assistance to read some words and to use
the Table of Contents, Glossary, Read More, Internet Sites,
and Index sections of the book.

Printed in the United States of America in North Mankato, Minnesota.
092013   007764CGS14

Table of Contents

4

I Am Kind

I treat people with kindness. I show the world that I care. I don't bully!

People's feelings
are important. I am nice
to everyone. Kids who bully
choose to pick on others.

I know how it feels to be teased. I don't want others to feel like that. Kids who bully don't care who they hurt.

I Show that I Care

I look out for people. Kids who bully only watch out for themselves.

I say thank you when friends, family, and others are nice to me. Kids who bully don't care about manners.

I care about keeping
my friends. I forgive
and forget. Kids who bully
don't care about friendships.

I Care for the World

I care about my world.

I clean up after myself.

Kids who bully throw trash

for attention.

18

Volunteering is a way
to care. I feel good
when I volunteer.
Kids who bully don't think
about supporting others.

I Have a Big Heart

I care about my world
and everyone in it.
That's why I'll never bully.

Glossary

attention—the interest of others; bullies act out so others notice them or take interest in them

bully—to be mean to someone else over and over again

forgive—to stop feeling angry at someone

manners—a kind, polite way of talking to and treating others

support—to help and encourage someone

volunteer—to help without being paid

Read More

Concord, Juliet. *I Am Kind.* Kids of Character. New York: Gareth Stevens Publishing, 2011.

Marshall, Shelley. *Super Ben Writes a Letter: A Book about Caring.* Character Education with Super Ben and Molly the Great. Berkeley Heights, N.J.: Enslow Publishers, 2010.

Thomas, Isabel. *Caring.* Dealing with Feeling. Chicago: Heinemann, 2013.

Internet Sites

FactHound offers a safe, fun way to find Internet sites related to this book. All of the sites on FactHound have been researched by our staff.

Here's all you do:

Visit *www.facthound.com*

Type in this code: 9781476540702

Check out projects, games and lots more at
www.capstonekids.com

Index

Word Count: 157
Grade: 1
Early-Intervention Level: 12

Editorial Credits
Jeni Wittrock, editor; Juliette Peters, designer; Svetlana Zhurkin, media researcher;
Kathy McColley, production specialist; Sarah Schuette, photo stylist;
Marcy Morin, photo scheduler

Photo Credits
Capstone Studio: Karon Dubke, cover, 4, 6, 8, 10, 12, 14, 18, 20; iStockphotos:
Steve Debenport, 16